Life doesn't bring us many old friends like

Midge

Adelaide Cummings

Earlier books by Adelaide Cummings

Poetry

Pastiche
Reprise
Finale
Zoo's Who *
Double Vision (*with Steve Best)*)
Grand Finale

Prose

Auguste Piccard (*biography*)**
The Challenge of the Seafloor **

Juvenile Fiction
<>

Adventure on the "*Cloud Nine*" ***
Mystery on Cape Cod

*   Dow-Jones Press
**   Houghton Mifflin
***   G.P. Putnam & Sons

Curtain Call
Even More Poems By

Adelaide Cummings

Art on front cover; Body is from a postcard of Follies Bergeres (Paris circa 1900) by Walery French (1883-1935). Face, inserted by Jeff Anderson, is that of the author at nineteen. Book cover by Jeffrey M. Anderson

Many of the poems included here have previously appeared in magazines, newspapers, periodicals or anthologies.No poem printed here may be reprinted without author's permission. All are copyrighted.

Introduction

How brief, the future, long, the past,
How short, the shadow I now cast.
How vast my love of life has been,
How inadequate, my pen.

Loving challenge, holding fast,
I've held at bay despair, dismay,
And yes, I guess it's fair to say,
Charged full-force into each day
As though it were my last.

Now rushing Time can almost stun,
All those battles not yet won,
Temptations that I failed to shun,
Much to rue, look back upon.
Yet flowers, music, hours of play,
Work that I love have graced my day.
Children, friends, my piece of sod
Make mine an unpaid *debt to God.*

For some on earth, dawn's just begun.
<u>My</u> dusk has drawn, day nearly done.
Fear of the future? I have none,
For strong, the Arm I lean upon,
And glorious, the setting sun..

Read, and as you turn each page,
Journey with me, youth-to-age.

Problem

Oh dear, oh dear, the guests are here!
   Too, six o'clock is drawing near.
Must I remind them, make it clear
   To take things as they find them?
Do you think they'll understand,
   When hunger drives them blind,
That, when basking on the sand,
   Food's last thing on my mind?

Little Sister

"My big brother loves to banter.
   Now he's saying there's no Santa.
He's turning into such a bore!
   I *saw* Santa at the store.

He'd better drop his fibbing role.
   His stocking? Filled with lumps of coal!
That's what he'll get for being so mean,
   And when he starts to fuss, complain,
I might share my tangerine,
   But not my candy cane!"

Bounty

Steer clear of me. Can't you see
   I have a loosened hinge?
Hear me say "Don't block my way.
   No duties must impinge."
My peach tree's showering peaches,
   Enough to make me cringe,
And I lust for home-made pie crust
   On my yearly cooking binge.
Don't stand in line! Avoid the crunch.
   There'll be time, for I've this hunch:
Pie for dinner, breakfast, lunch!

Oh yes, I'm putting on a show.
   (I don't do things by halves, you know!)
Still, next week stay out of reach
   Should you, unwitting, murmur "Peach".

June

Today's a day to wander
   On sunlit paths and sand.
It's not a day to squander
   On tasks too near at hand.
The fences sag with roses,
   Blueberries dot the land.
The rule good sense imposes?
   "Obey your heart's command."

That's why you'll find me, out of reach,
   With a book, here on the beach.

Enough!

Cranky kids, the loss of pet,
   Nagging woes prone to upset,
Almost any pesky thing
   Will head folks straight to counseling.
In my day, when not in clover,
   All our woes we just *got over.*
We did not collapse, go slack,
   We got ourselves right back on track.

Newspapers dish out dreadful junk,
   What's become of good old spunk?
You're bound to meet with trouble, strife,
   But other folks can't fix your life.
If Fate should strew your path with boulders,
   It's up to you. Throw back your shoulders!
It's glorious fun to strive, compete,
   Standing tall *on our own feet.*

Imaginative

I have always been the kind
   Who excels at dodging work.
Trust me. I can always find
   Creative ways to shirk!

First Things First

Sweep the floor? Oh not today!
   A noble poem is on the way.
Collect the garbage? I refuse!
   This might scare away my Muse.
The very most that I am able?
   Well, (perhaps) to set the table.

Capice?

Dear friends whom I hug, embrace,
Read and heed.
I need space.
When door is closed, don't think me rude.
What my work needs is
Solitude.
I, who love to laugh and play,
Soon enough will join the fray.
Urge me not, I pray, to stray.
I love it when you come my way,
But not today!

Gardener's Prayer

Accept my thanks, Up There on High.
We've worked together, you and I,
Making lovely what was bare,
That rose that so perfumes the air,
That noble tree I planted there
To offer shelter to the birds.
My thanks can't be expressed in words.
I've friends to share
Results of all my work and care.

This makes me wonder how folks dare
Not believe in answered prayer.

Then and Now

Then

" Elope? Oh no! I want a veil,
A long lace train to trail,
And lots of well-dressed wedding guests
Who'll send us china plates with crests!"

Now

"You're suggesting we *elope?*
Listen, dope. Back up!
Life's just begun. So much more fun
If we just shack up!"

Memory

So many things that I know well,
  (Far too many here to tell,)
Seem to vanish, slip away.
       Where do they go?
       I don't know!
I confess, when they regress,
  They too often cause distress.

  Do I owe a tax to I.R.S.,
     Or is recollection lax?
We're told that memory is selective,
  But what I need is a *detective*,
     To help me find lost facts.

Hark!

Write that poem, sing that song!
  Shout out at every civic wrong.
Criticism we can weather
  Because we've got our act together.
This didn't happen overnight,
  But we've had time to get things right.
Old folks today are wiser, stronger,
  For don't forget, we're living longer.

I contend we have more fun.
  (We've finished things Youth's just begun.)
We're not beset with swings of mood,
  We've been imbued with fortitude.
We play, we hike, we like to swim,
  Enjoy our workouts at the gym,
Done with committees, done with school,
  No longer slaves to fashion's rule,
And best of all, I'm pleased to say,
  Care not one whit what others say.

So let Old Age's praise be sung.
  We've earned release for pen and tongue.
Hurrah! The curtain's not yet rung.
  I ask you! Who craves being <u>young</u>?

Death Knell

Oh how I've loved the ball game,
   Such a treat to see!
But I despair. It isn't fair,
   Once more they've raised the fee.
You know of course, what surely follows.
   Crowds of fans in hills and hollows
 Resent those bums, their piles of dollars.
   So what to do? Is this the key,
To switch our viewing to T.V?
   But watch those salaries escalating.
   You've just improved their T.V. rating!

And so farewell, each greedy rube.
   Cost is now a major menace.
Henceforth I will switch the tube
      To tennis.
May you, in pocketbook-distress,
   Make many <u>many</u> millions
      Less!

Heed

Hear my appeal.
(I'm viewed as older than I _feel_.)
I won't be senile for *a while*
And do not have dementia,.
And so, good host,
Raise no glass high until I die,
Then toast me *in absentia.*

Sound Advice

"The world's a book. If you don't travel,
You're reading just one page."
So said Saint Augustine, the sage.
But let's not cavil. I'll engage
Until I've reached far greater age.

Interpretation

"Sow the tempest, reap the storm,"
An expression deemed the norm.
It doesn't make me tip *my* hat.
Not one bit of fun in that!
With both my hands I grasp for pleasure.
Joy's not alloy,
It's *treasure!*

Encounter

A robin high up in a tree
Looked down, turned up his beak at me.
"The whole world listens when I sing.
<u>You're</u> not much good at anything!
The things you do are non-essential,
Nothing I'd call 'consequential'.
Another fact, not incidental?
You're not even <u>ornamental</u>."

Enraged at this attack I'd weathered,
I vowed to have him caged, de-feathered.
The very thought made spirits zoom.
I'd pile those feathers *on his tomb!*
Nothing in this world could save him!
(But then he sang, and I forgave him).

Passé

Our century's clearly not the one
    For gentry.
I doubt that it will ever see
    Re-entry.

Solicitor

You, intruder I could slap,
    Who uninvited, ruins my nap
With calls I don't condone,
    You won't prevail, call's bound to fail,
Reach me next by U.S. mail
    And steer clear of my phone!

Tilt

When placed upon the Scale of Life,
    Laughter outweighs pain.
Should we cavil at the price
    Or just enjoy net gain?

Pay Heed!

Go away! I'm reading!
Disturb me only if you're
Bleeding!

"I've always intended…"

You say you've "deep poetic thought"
  You "don't dare to put on paper".
But noble thought, if left uncaught,
    Is nought but vapor.
Why not give that thought release?
  You'll earn a satisfying peace
If you share with others, via ink,
  Those penetrating thoughts you think.

Guilt

Would there were way to hide my shame,
  But I alone must bear the blame.
Considered 'well brought-up' and trained,
  My sinful move goes far to prove
    Values exert no pull.
(This might explain *his* tank, now drained,
    My empty one, now full.)

Unfair

"Beauty lies in beholder's eyes",
  A line to make me smolder,
Most cruel joke in all the book.
  My bloke won't even take a look,
Now that I've grown older.

In the Same Boat

I sympathize with my great-gran,
  The one who's just past two.
You see, I'm finding button-holes
  Extremely hard to do.

So, what the deuce, let's both have fun
  And leave the pesky things undone.
Folks who bitch and fuss and yelp,
  Why don't they just *pitch in and help?*

National Treasure

Let our English language <u>dominate,</u>
  Intrusive others put in tethers!
Let's stand firm and boldly state:
  "Don't ruffle Eagle's feathers!"

Southern Belles

Way back then, our views were slanted.
  (Few radios, and no T.Vs.)
We stayed near where we were planted,
  And in the land that drops its g's,
We had one major aim. To please.

Night Thoughts on the Beach

The sea is murmurous, laps the shore,
   Gone, its recent thunderous roar.
Stars shimmer high in heaven's dome
   On moon-drenched strand, now edged in foam,
And standing out there all alone,
   Those distant stars become my own.
They, like the sea, blend into me.
   I'm akin to every grain of sand
Now running idly through my hand,
   To creatures deep out in that sea,
To Space, to all eternity,
   To all that's beautiful, diverse,
To the music of the universe.

That's when you'll hear my simple plea:
   "Oh Higher Power, you who preserve it,
Make poor worthless Man deserve it!"

Listen!

It's simple, what I want to do,
Just go out with you!
I know that home's a pleasure dome,
But I get beset with urge to roam!
Food would taste so really great
If I hadn't cooked it.
Might not be able to get a table?
I've already booked it!

Dissonance

How harsh they fall upon the ear,
Words we *do not want to hear.*
I'll call a line to your attention
That others find sublime,
One I loathe, and hate to mention..
"Had we but world enough, and time". *

^ *Andew Marvel. "To His Coy Mistress".*

No Time to Waste

How often widowers re-wed
With a haste like Hamlet's mother.
No empty house, no empty bed,
Just one- spouse- to-another.

Bonus

Oh the pleasure that they foster,
   Friends who adorn my friendship-roster!
I have found in their society
   All forms of variety.
(Two I like a lot are <u>bland,</u>
   Cool, the life they fashion.
I, whose blood ran fierce and hot,
   Doubt that they've known passion.)
Yet I have others, bolder friends,
   Who burn the candle at both ends.
One wins ribbons with her rose,
   (One hates the one who won it!)
Some attend to serious prose,
   Some prefer 'whodunit'.
Some like the waltz, some do the Twist,
   Golf's a sport some can't resist,
     Others shun it.
   (But don't forget this sound advice:
Friendship can demand a price
   In loyalty and sacrifice.)

Oh bless you all, the weak, the bold,
   You bring spice to growing old!

Bargain?

Here's a fact that you should measure.
 Children take a frightful bite
  From leisure.
Each one thinks he has a right
 To all your time and treasure.
Yet almost every girl or boy
 Repays a thousand times in joy.
(But oh, beware! Your right to praise them
 Depends a lot on how you raise them.)

There's this to weigh, and then there's that,
 And would there were an answer pat.
Yes, life is brief, a fragile bubble,
 Is joy not <u>worth</u> the cost of trouble?

How you answer will depend
 On what you deem life's major end.

Choice

 I'm undone.
How bumpy is the road, and graveled!
 You see, I took the one
  Most traveled.

Listen, Learn

"Great-grans, must I now implore you
    To eat what's put before you?
 In my day, we did!
    (Of course we very often hid
The okra we were meant to eat
    Behind our meat!)
 Fooling parents was a feat,
    And candy? Just for special treat.
 Too, we had no Pepsi, or its ilk,
    What we drank was milk.

The dental bill that I've just paid
    Was for your molars, some decayed.
But me? Oh yes, I thank my fate
    For a fact beyond debate.
Note the smile that I bequeath.
    You see, Great Gran has *all her teeth!*"

Erosion

Outright evil we all shun,
    But our noble deeds? Too few.
It's not the wrongs that we have done,
    But the good we failed to do.
Is it too late? Can't we eschew
    Our lapses and begin anew?

Down with recrimination, sighing.
    Not one thing to lose by trying!

Safe

I, who love to dance and frolic,
Will never be an
Alcoholic.
Heed my prediction.
Folks don't die of stroke or colic
When their addiction's
CHOCKoholic.

Explain it!

It's <u>weird.</u>
My car keys just disappeared!
Will angry friends refuse to speak?
The *very thing* occurred last week!

Plan

We've been told that it is best
To rise up early, eat, get dressed.
But I, who linger long in bed,
Avoid the hurly-burly,
Pick up a book I haven't read,
And, as I peruse each page,
In lofty thoughts engage.

Now don't protest or cause me rage!
Don't **you** long to reach this stage?

My Choice

In my aging rocking-chair
  I often sit and stare.
A fire burns bright. The falling light
  Casts shadows everywhere.
At this well-known "witching hour",
  The past asserts its power.
Then old folks feel lonely,
  And I don't understand.
The memories I carry
  Are always near at hand.
They never seem to dim or fade,
  I'm free to pick decade.
Will it be childhood in its glory,
  Or middle-age, or old?
Which, most cherished story,
  Which will best unfold?
Perhaps, when my own children
  Filled my arms and heart?
Oh hooray! I think today
  That's just the place to start.

More

Such a satisfactory day!
From the start, things went my way.
   I made myself clean up the dishes,
Had lunch outdoors and on a tray,
   Gave in to all my slothful wishes,
Packed my worries far away.
   An idle hour? I filled the gap,
Read a book, took a nap,
   Then off to sunny swim.
Next this undeserving sinner
   Got herself asked out to dinner,
(Wore her most becoming sweater
   For this handsome man!)
      Will life get better?
      Doubt it can.

Delusion.

We've been lent Earth. Here, as guest
   We savor what's made manifest,
Its oceans and its bowers.
   I, who have relished and embellished
My little bit with flowers,
   Though not imbued with rectitude,
Offer heartfelt gratitude
   For all we *think* is ours.

Near-Miss

I'm under siege, or worse, a curse!
   I've mislaid or lost my purse!
My lipstick, comb, and sun-screen too,
   My dates for fêtes and rendez-vous,
The market list for soon-due guest,
   Phone numbers shared at my request,
Recipes, my household keys,
   Prescription for my cough and sneeze,
A tiny packet of detergent,
   Long list for assistance urgent,
New shoelaces for my boots,
   Two packs of sugar-substitutes,
Gum and Tums, a tube of lotion,
   A pill to take for airplane motion,
When did I let down my guard?
   How live without my credit card,
Checkbook and PIN for A.T.M?
   My life's reduced to pure mayhem!
Of cell-phone I am now bereft,
   Victim of a heartless theft.
Face it, *I've got nothing left!*
    ....
Thank you, thank you, great Creator!
     But I declare,
    In the *refrigerator?*
I'm showing mental wear-and-tear?
   Of course I didn't put it there!
It's either a malicious elf,
   Or else it got there *by itself!*

Maiden Voyage
(Sailor suitor)

He
"Persuading her sure cost me bribes,
   But I'm not getting such great vibes."

She
"Of course I'm wailing!
   I do find it so unfair
To get beset with mal-de-měr
   Because I'm not a Neptune-daughter.
But if those waves would give us quarter
   I *might* like sailing..
      .. Sorta."

Me
I'd call this day one to forget!
Will she try again? Care to bet?

History Revisited

Standing tall by village green,
  An ancient church can still be seen,
Erected by a sturdy band
  On what was then King George's land.
And today we celebrate the date,
  That distant Seventeen- O- Eight *.

Men wore frock coats in those days,
  Women, pelisses, corsets, stays..
Twice turned, an hour-glass would determine
  Length of two- hour Hell -fire sermon.

Moved, and placed on Village Green,
  This church has so much history seen!
It was Paul Revere who fashioned well
  The church's big melodious bell.
(For special times, parishioners , kneeling,
  Can hear today that old bell pealing.)
.

Time marches on, the years roll past,
  But the little church was built to last.
Through Revolution, battle, strife,
  It played its part in village life,
A place for solace, shelter, care,
  For hope, stability and prayer.

Today, with past and present blended,
  The church has grown, outreach extended,
Every service well attended.
  Impervious to the tooth of Time,
None could deem it past its prime.
  This little church with spire so tall
Has seen kings topple, empires fall.
  Still it endures, so heed its call.
With open arms, it welcomes all.

300 year anniversary. 1st Congregational Church.
Main Street, Falmouth ,Massachusetts.
****

Patriot's Wife

"Oh no, he wasn't drafted,
    But <u>chose</u> to go
    To fight in far Iraq.
Children, I really do not *know*
    When he's coming back."

I didn't want them filled with fear,
    Not one whiff.
    Note how I avoided
      Saying "if".

'Teen Tragedy

Who's telling you that I am blue?
  That's not *altogether* true,
    But patient I am not.
Oh, disappointment hurts the throat!
  How did he <u>ever</u> get my vote?

You see, my brand-new beau *forgot.*
  He sent no birthday note,
  And oh, I'll make him rue it.
When next I see him I'll shout "Scat!"
  Watch me hand that guy his hat,
Give knuckle raps and sound out Taps!
    I'm going to do it!
    …Well, perhaps.

Hooked

I'm, gadget-prone, cannot resist
  Adding new ones to my list.
(Try to name one that I've missed!)
  None of them can make me balk,
Some tote up the miles I walk,
  To itchy ailments promise cure,
Provide new-fangled fishing lure,
  Tell me if my water's pure,
Or what's the outdoor temperature.

Buying them's an endless chore,
  And too, they take up so much space!
My closet chaos? A disgrace.
  When I meet Saint Peter face to face
He'll give up *on a hopeless case.*

Will He ?

Oh yes, I caulked the leak.
My boat is bobbing on the brine
     As we speak.
Why not cast off my mooring line?
     I have chores too bleak!
But everything could work out fine
     Next week.

Still, the southwest wind's prevailing
     On this almost perfect day,
And I should go a-sailing
     To somewhere far away,
To Mandalay or far Cathay,
     Perhaps a cove in Bay Biscay.

Oh, I could go this very day,
     But boring duties block my way.
Skip them? Relationships might fray..
          O woe!
     Anyhow, I'm sure to go
          Someday!

Air Travel

"Fly the friendly skies."
That ad's eliminated!
This should come as no surprise
For a promise so outdated.
"Adieu" to pillow, peanuts, blanket.
If it's a perk they're going to yank it.
You must change your attitude
And plan to make your visits nude,
For be assured a grim-faced hag
Will demand a fee for every bag.
No use to weep. They'll give no quarter.
Now they charge you for your water.
My yen to fly? See how it melts.
Next, they'll charge us for seat belts!

Disillusion

Was he unflawed, this well-read man
  Whose voice was soft as butter?
Oh his verses! How they'd scan,
  And cause my heart to flutter!.
I thought of interests we might share,
  But alas, alas, life's so unfair!
In my garden, standing there
  Amid my well-loved roses,
I saw him shrug and then declare
  "I've never cared for posies."

How I bless a kindly Fate!
I might have found this out *too late.*

Hurry!

Doctor, act!
Take my last dime..
Just extract
The tooth of Time!

Salvage

Oh dear!
"Occasion" verse? I yearn to curse!
Will I ever learn to turn
Sow's ear
To silken purse?

First Love

Why is it that I still remember
    One kiss in the dark?
Why does it still burn, that ember,
    Still glow, that spark?
I've wrinkles now etched on my face,
    Emblems on Time's chart,
But enfolded in old fragrant lace,
    That memory stands apart.

Aging

Alas, it now becomes your fate
    To see your face deteriorate.
Another thought that troubles, sickens?
    The way your once-slim body thickens.
Too, you must fight a dire depravity,
    The slow, relentless Law of Gravity.

Balance, now a liability,
    Has decimated your agility.
But dry those tears. Cease to brood,
    Buck up! Change your attitude.
Your hip, your knees, have been *renewed.*

    Imbued with grace, again elastic,
Grateful for these measures drastic,
    Farewell to days when you were spastic.
Good as new, *you now are plastic!*

Crossed Wires

She

What a mistake!
I asked him for his mother's sake,
And he turned out to be a *rake*.
(Even when we played Nintendo
He found a way for innuendo!)
Alas, alas, his clumsy passes,
What a blunder!
Does his mother know? I wonder..

A pedigree's no guarantee.
A lesson sadly learned by me.

He

I do trust Mom, but you'll agree,
That dame <u>thrust</u> <u>herself</u> on me!
This cold fish is not my dish,
How soon can I flee?

Mamma

Of course I never interfere,
All I do is gently *steer*.
I'll observe this girl. Is she the one?
Does she <u>deserve</u> my son?

Recession

Uncertain future? Who's to say?
   But why let fears confound us?
We've time to read, to think, to play,
   And glorious things surround us.
Thus I do not blink at Adam's 'curse'.
   Things could be, I truly think,
      A whole lot worse!

Tread With Care

Back in the Thirties, ladies bold
   Were told of "woman's place".
Home was the realm where hers, the helm.
   Let no "big notions" overwhelm!

If you agree, then dodge my path,
   Lest I play out that pent-up wrath.

Overworked

When lost, her time for playing,
   This tired, misunderstood one
Prays that you'll stop saying
   "Have a good one!"

Emptied

How complex is the human heart!
   We build on what sets us apart,
Find the thing that makes us sing,
     Garner information
On where we fit in life's equation.

In verse I've always found release
   From tribulation, woe,
For sense of joy, for inner peace.
   So when it's time to go,
All of me's out there to see,
   Nothing's left to know.
Thus friend or foe, or curious gaper,
   You'll find me there, out bare on paper.
Know I'll exhort you, from my hearse,
   "Get to know me via my verse".

Voyage

On many roads, through many rooms
   We make our way through life,
And all about, temptation looms,
   The piper plays his fife.
Yet each of us is given chance
   To weep or to rejoice.
What to do? It's up to you.
   Join the piper's dance?
The answer's clear, so mark it here.
   Heed your inner voice!

Secret Revealed

To satisfy the menfolk well,
  As Grandma was aware,
Required a certain glorious smell
  To permeate the air.

That smell, my friends, was not Chanel
  Nor Paté Foie Gras.
Oh no, no, no! I'll gladly tell
  What enraptured Grandpapa.

The smell that captured rugged men,
  Turned each one into mouse,
Was the smell of baking bread
  Wafted through the house.

How it drew them! Ooh la la!,
  And just between us few,
The smell that <u>felled</u> my Grandpapa
  Will still work well for you.

Then

Once, with footsteps light as feather,
  I laughed at distance, time and weather.
I relished hail or rainy span,
  Earthquake in far-away Japan,
Squall on Scotland heather,
  Heat wave in Mandalay, Rangoon,
And most of all, the Taj Mahal
  Beneath a rounded moon.
Oh those wondrous trips, far flung!
  More lay ahead, for we were young.

All these events occurring
  When life's calendar read "June"
Were not a waste, though aftertaste
  Was sure to vanish soon.
For as time melts, it gives no warning,
  No extra hours are strewn.
It's then the Piper *halts* his tune,
  That joyous, soaring boon.
It's then we rue what's all too true.
  How far away, the morning,
    How long gone is noon!

Block

No poem came my way today,
  And yes, I'm left bereft.
My muse gave up and went away.
  Do you suppose she'll *stay?*
Summer parties, fireworks, fêtes,
  One barely ends, the next awaits.
Alas, alas, just as I feared,
  All this frolic interfered,
And I, so often pulled two ways,
  Who always seek the flawless phrase,
Am split asunder, left to wonder
  How to survive this phase.

  Can I resist dilemma's twist,
Be wise, and compromise?
  Brought on by me, this awful loss
Leaves me spent, to turn and toss.

Mortality

Oh how I have loved the stars
   That blaze up there on high.
But see! There's one now shooting
   Across the spangled sky.
It makes me sad, who should be glad,
   And here's the reason why.
I find the thought uprooting,
   That even stars can die.

New Mantra

"Change" is the magic word today,
   Change, the master-key.
Change will blow the past away,
   Change is Sesame.

Why does that word not work for me,
   Who so prefers stability?
I, who once was brave and bold
   Must face the fact I'm growing old!

Lost To Posterity

My vanished thought? Oh it was dandy!
   (Alas, I had no pencil handy.)

Hard Truth

What an ideal day to play!
  My spirits sing and soar and zing,
And I feel up to anything.
  First I'll complete this one dull chore,
Then set out to play, explore.
  But dear, oh dear, just as I feared,
My energy just disappeared,
  I can't do one thing more!

Decrepitude, how I reject it!
  Why did I somehow not expect it?
Surely this is not deserved.
  It's one of life's most cruel jokes,
Just the kind that Satan pokes,
  And one that I had thought reserved
    For *other* folks.

Authority

Up there strumming on her harp,
  (Her mind about to warp,)
She grabbed an angel by the wing:
  "I've got this quirk. I like to <u>work.</u>
Heaven would be so much cosier!
  Please! I'll do most <u>anything,</u>
And you'd *love* my ambrosia!"

What happened next? An angel-glare.
  "When you climb the Golden Stair
You earn Perpetual Rest.
  Novice! It would not surprise us
If you tried to *organize* us!
  Don't waste my time. Cease to carp.
Stop causing trouble. On the double,
  Get back to that harp!"

Ill Defined

Why do they call it "sweet repose"?
  Heaven knows
We should live life up on our toes!
  I want no fraction of inaction.
Devoid of challenge, battles, foes,
  I'd call this "recipe for woes."

Shopping Shock

In Neiman-Marcus, dressed to kill,
  I wandered, seeking Boutique Thrill.
How remarked on, my allure,
  How staid my footstep, steady, sure,
Sprayed and upswept, my coiffure,
  And my new purchase? Haute couture!

Folks note my elegance, my grace.
  (Oh, I belong in such a place!)
But soon good-will is blunted, stunted.
  Hear me wail, affronted, tense
From this Retail Experience.

Is he beserk, that uptight clerk?
  What kind of world does he inhabit,
    This rigid rabbit?
Observe his glare, his frown, his stare
  That questions *what I'm doing there.*
It hurts my pride, my glamor hampers.
  (I shouldn't have tried to buy some Pampers!)

Point of View

Prone to always made the case
  That we'll perfect the human race,
The future's one that I embrace.
  Fears I put to rout and chase,
Just let me face old age with grace!

Puzzled

Two egrets out there on the pond
   It's clear to see have bonded,
And since to me one's like another,
   I wonder how they found each other.
Is it that birds, like you and me,
   Have individual chemistry?
Does this apply to cormorant,
   To elephant and lowly ant?

Our vanity has reached new peak
   When we deem ourselves unique.
My point-of-view has been defective.
   What I require's a new perspective.
Those birds reveal life's broader span
   And show how limited is Man.
They chart how very small our part
   In one big Universal Heart.

Looking Back

There's far too much newspaper "spin"
  About the troubled times we're in
That experts label "mild recession".
  Each of us should try regression
Toward what is termed the Great Depression.
  No agencies were there to aid,
No Medicare, no Medicaid.
  Yet folks did not concede defeat.
Some sold apples on the street,
  Did their best to aid each other,
Tried to spare a dime for brother.
  With so little cause for glee,
We shared camaraderie,
  Dispensed with pointless woe, despair,
And then at last, came up for air!

Let's shut each mouth and square each chin,
  Then *dig out* from what we're in,
And relegate complaint to shelves.
  God helps those who help themselves!

Amazement

"Gran, how *can* you be so merry?
   You have no I-pod, no Blackberry,
And never ever take a look
     At Face Book.
Too, now that you no longer jog,
   You ought to Blog!

What you need is <u>me</u> for tutor,
   To get the most from your computer.
The things you miss! It's such a pity.
   You never watch "Sex and the City"!
Gran, when your boring day is done,
   What do you find to do *for fun?*
Still, if you're sad you sure don't show it,
   So maybe life is not <u>all</u> bad
     For just a poet!"

Unforgiving

I grieve!
Will we ever find reprieve
From what was loosed by Adam, Eve?
Bankruptsy, boils, the mean boll-weevil,
   All accrue from that first evil.
How could we even think to pardon
   Folks who enjoyed, for home,
     A garden?

Challenge

When young I gave no thought to pain,
 I'd plunge into a towering wave,
Be hurled back onto sand,
  Then return again, again,
  A self-imposed command.

It's not much fun when we achieve
  What we want, with too much ease.
It's best when life can toss and spin us,
  Put us to the test,
For this fires up within us
  Urge to do our best,
To have our wisest sayings quoted,
  And most of all, our passage noted.

Life's challenges should not be spurned.
 I plan to live with vigor, zest.
And when it comes, have **earned** my rest.

Command

I leapt from bed.
"Hooray, hooray!
I get Fido from the vet today."
(There in the waiting- room I read
"Sit! Stay").

City Dweller

Oh dear, oh dear!
The next-door penthouse is so near,
And that awful neighbor, Mack!
Do you suppose that he's on <u>crack?</u>
The fellow's crude. Still, he's stunning.
(It's those workouts, all that running.)
Oh, don't shut the curtain. Slide the track!
He's out there *nude,* and sunning
On his <u>back!</u>

Recipe

"Boil in oil, then slather butter."
That's when I 'm apt to hear you mutter
"Calories will take some battening.
Only Southerners can make
Vegetables fattening!"

Woe

"You should step out in something *new ",*
This comment? All too true.
I <u>have</u> new garments on my racks,
What *is* it each one lacks?
When my clothes require retiring,
See them there, in stacks,
I find how hard it is to part
With ratty jeans, frayed denim,
Knowing from the very start
The fun that I've had in 'em.

The parting leaves me close to tears..
Those new clothes? It will take *years!*

Half-Empty Glass

"What a treat, this perfect day,
   And oh that bird there on my feeder!"
But she just looked and turned away,
   "Today's a <u>weather breeder</u>!"

Will you love your life or rue it?
   Much depends on *how you view it.*

Nostalgia

Neighbor, I confess, alas,
   That I am less than keen
On your brand-new mow-machine.
   It's noisy, and it uses <u>gas</u>.
I miss the hand-pushed one, its *whirr,*
   Oh the memories it could stir!
(Garden parties on the lawn
   That turned to dancing until dawn.)

I do so wonder who's to blame..
   Grass today *doesn't smell the same!*

Reprieve

It's just too bad, and yes, I'm sad!
  There's little hope to muster.
Oh that so misleading ad
  That promised "added luster".
It makes me hot beneath my collar.
  This is no year to waste one dollar.
That empty claim! I *look the same!*
  It makes my mind begin to boggle,
    This <u>hornswoggle</u>!

But wait! Here is what the label speaks:
  "*Movie stars* all use these jars.
Can you expect, in just six weeks
  Youth to recapture and restore?
    Buy ten jars more!"

        Oh rapture!
It's clear this label tells the truth,
  So I am off to Beauty Booth.
Look to your laurels, movie stars!
  I'm starting with a <u>dozen</u> jars!

Quiz

Two presidents sought a road to peace
  To bring about war's ending.
Which one was it chose lend-lease,
  Which, sacrifice-through-spending?

Locale

"Mom, your diction misses being first-rate
  Because you don't <u>enunciate</u>.
It has brought us near to tears,
  What we've endured for all these years.
We are kind, and not too snippy
  When you call that state "Miss-<u>sippy</u>",
Another sample? This example.
  It can almost drive us blind,
The way you butcher "Never mind".
  There's absolutely no excuse.
A simple phrase in common use!

Our patience won't encounter drought,
  We'll keep at it, won't resign,
We'll amend your South-in-mouth.
  We'll teach you not to say "Nem'mine".

Atlanta

Did he really think he'd win,
  Hitler, that German vermin,
And don't you think he must be kin
  To General Sherman?

English

My reputation faces <u>smother.</u>
  I thought I'd clearly said one thing,
And found I'd said another.
    (How could one deleted comma
      Cause such drama?)

My love of grammar? Yes, it's hearty,
    Though sometimes I'm the guilty party.
Yet hear me urge, (no pause or stammer,)
    That we <u>all</u> upgrade our grammar.
      Why the clamor?
Down with resistance! I can vow
  Our mother tongue requires assistance
    <u>Now.</u>

Blessing

Were Fate to say "I'll do my part,
  So choose one blessing a la carte,
Firelight's what I'd choose.
  Friends are what a fire requires,
And oh, the poems it inspires!
  That's why it tops my chart.

This blessing all our senses hones.
  Firelight more than warms the bones,
    It warms the heart.

Green Goddess

Alas, alas, I curse the Fates.
    (I rate for gift, some After Eights.)
Fine, until my best chum vaunts,
    Then flaunts what she discloses.
Is she one great big pain, or not !
    Here is what that <u>plain</u> girl got.
One dozen long-stemmed roses!

Diner's Dilemma

Oh dear, oh dear, I feel dejected.
    This meal's not quite what I expected,
But his looks great!
    Why do I always salivate
For what's on my near-neighbor's plate?

But see him glare, then stare at mine,
    He can't seem to stop!
Would it be too out of line?
    Could I ask him to <u>swap</u>?

Insistence

"Memory is guardian of all things",
        So says Cicero.
What sort of comfort this thought brings
        I do not know.
This worries me down to my shoes.
    The very thought brings on the blues.
There are memories that I *want* to lose.
    Grant me the right to pick and choose!

Bear Up

If your life extends past normal range,
   Accept as <u>fact</u> what you won't change.
Just dismiss it. Pay the price
   For friends and their unsought advice.
They find it risky, your open fire,
   Tell you at what hour to retire,
Feel sure that just one whiskey toddy
   Will cure every ailment in your body,
Point out your daily huge mistake
   (All those pills that you <u>don't</u> take.)
Most of all, they take delight
   In telling you *what poems to write.*
They put your patience to the test
   Via countless subjects they suggest.

      It's a waste of time.
That's why I'm telling them in rhyme
   "I love you all, and your attention,
But there is something I should mention.
   At my age, I've lost <u>retention.</u>
All those suggestions that you give?
   They slip right through my mental sieve.

Perhaps my life needs re-arranging,
   But old, set ways? *Too late for changing!"*

Hands Off

It seems to me we've gone too far.
  We're not the universe's czar.
To me it strikes a note that jars
  When we try to seize its keys.
I have no wish to live on Mars,
  Or colonize the seas,
 And I, who glory in Earth's splendor,
  Don't want control of human gender.

With urge to tinker we are cursed.
  Why not fix our own world first?
We have yet to find solution
  For depredation and pollution.
The <u>universe</u> is not our biz.
  I vote to leave it as it is!

Orders

When you talk too much
I lose it.
You have the right to silence.
Use it.

Overkill

We're out to dine. Supplied with wine,
   The best the restaurant can provide,
      I scan the chart.
A dozen choices, a la carte.
   But heaven knows they gild the rose!
I've seldom read such purple prose.
   The fish they say is "gratiné"
There's no such thing as plain soufflé.
   Chicken? Stuffed with viands unknown
And I groan at titles overblown.

   How hyperbole can soar!
Choosing's now become a chore.
   But a haughty waiter's standing there
Tapping pencil, by my chair,
   So I must choose. Do I dare?
Oh, what the hell! I've nerve to spare,
   "Bring me, please, a plain steak, rare."

Correction

"Why don't you use your head?" they yell,
   And I should heed them well.
But I have rules, do understand,
   That bind me in their spell.

One special rule I've set apart,
   And followed from the start:
"Forget the duties head had planned,
   And listen to your heart".

Dilemma

My daily crossword makes me think,
   There's no doubt about it.
Into gloom I'd surely sink,
   Were I to do without it.
From dictionary help I shrink,
   And, my fingers stained with ink,
When the puzzle's done, I shout it.

I know whose State Flower is magnolia,
   Can name the capitol of Mongolia,
That "esse" is Latin for "to be",
   That a needle case is an "etui".
All these facts, and myriads more
   Are minutiae that I adore,
Yet just one thing dims my elation.
   How work them into conversation?

Plea

Although I love each blazing leaf,
   Autumn's stay is all too brief.
Because departure's far too soon,
   Confer on me one major boon.

Winter, hold off one more week!
   That is all I dare bespeak.
Don't allow your heart to harden.
   Spare this last rose in my garden!

Repaid

I think I've now become a part
   Of my garden's heart.
I've planted roses, flowering vine,
   Baby's Breath and Columbine,
      And, don't forget,
Raised them all from cold, bare sod,
   Helped by fertilizer, God,
      And my own sweat.

You'd like to bet I'd shun the neighbor
   Who did not laud results of labor?
I wouldn't mind, or find this hard!
   Gardening *is its own reward*.

Tables Turned

"Momma dear, we're near despair.
  We don't like the clothes you wear!
Those tennis shorts, your bathing-suit,
  Do dredge up a substitute.
We were not expecting, at this stage,
  Clothes too young for folks your age!
Why don't you try a closet-clearance?
  Mom, folks *judge you by appearance!*
We're not suggesting black or grey,
      But *red?*

That's all we care to say today.
  Think it over when in bed.
And that brings this to mind. We find
  You stay up far too late.
You ought to be in bed by eight."
    .. ..
      Ahem, ahem,
Is this the way I talked to *them?*
  It gives my spirits such a boost.
Chickens do come home to roost!

East, West

Travel's over, left behind,
  Riches of the heart and mind,
Friendships made, and ties that bind,
  But despite the lure of foreign ways
There's one strong pull my heart obeys.
  Home is where I'll end my days,

Heart's Voyage

Mine? Given to my children,
  To theirs, and then theirs too,
To friends and flowers and treasured pets,
  And I am finding true
That love is what our love begets,
  It bubbles up anew.
Higher than a mountain,
  It seems to have no crest,
This endless, spouting fountain,
  The heart's most welcome guest.

Lack

The world is large, my knowledge, scant.
  Would I had had a larger slant.
Oh if I could only widen
  Such a limited horizon!

Brat

You had a tantrum, Earth, today,
  Quite an awesome sight.
You let your temper have full sway,
  Caused us fright.
How you thundered, stormed and wept,
  Intent to have your say.
No way to halt, or intercept
  Until your dark clouds blew away.
But then at last, cajoled, beguiled,
  Rage assuaged, you smiled,
And straightaway, strong –minded child,
  That smile just made our day!

Definition

Life bestows on us a balm.
  Contentment blesses us with calm.
How I enjoy this treasured salve!
  (I don't want what I don't have.)

Nothing Changes

Invite me to your party
   And I'll worry; "What to wear?"
Of course this makes no sense at all.
   Who on earth would care?
But I stare into my looking-glass
   And tell myself I still might pass
For, well, not a <u>lot</u> past *eighty*.
   That's why what I wear tonight
Assumes importance weighty.

Decide

If you don't value your own time,
   Don't think that others will.
Should you decide to paint or rhyme,
   Then you've no time to kill.
Your time can be impinged upon
   In ways that make you cringe.
Although you won't believe it now,
   Time must be given sway.
As we grow older, how we grieve
   For golden hours we can't retrieve.
And chances slipped away.

All we're sure of is today.
   Grab it by the scruff,
Because someday you're sure to say:
   "Wish I'd had enough!"

.

Rebel

Today, I vow,
Care sits heavy on my brow,
And I know well the reason.
Clothes, they say, should not be worn
Out of season.

Here's a rule you must remember.
No white shoes worn in September!
Dress in wool past month of May?
Your sense of style has gone astray.

Whoever heard such tommyrot?
Is this a tease?
I wear anything I've got,
When I please!

If I choose, I'll <u>shed</u> my shoes.
(Will they see red at "Fashion News"?)
Too, <u>who</u>, I ask, hews to the letter,
And cold in June, omits a sweater?

Down with such rules! I state anew:
It's fools who <u>get</u> <u>dictated</u> <u>to</u>.

Do It Now

Has no-one told you? When you're old,
  Memories acquire a power
They never had before.
  These are things you should explore
Before it comes, that final hour
  When Life will slam the door.
So do it <u>now</u>. *Tote up your score!*

Repentance? Such a boring chore!
  (Yet Hell's what preachers all deplore,
And Heaven could prove *a deadly bore.)*
So before you leave this golden shore,
  <u>Press that pedal to the floor!</u>

Both Cases
(Youth and Age)

"We young ones feel we need a sedative
   Because old folks are so <u>repetitive,</u>
Somehow unable to keep score,
   Telling and re-telling
 What's been told before.
This should rate an o-piate!
   Want to know what we most hate?
The way you all *pontificate.*''

,,,,,,,,,,,,,,,,,,,·

"Why is it that you don't rejoice
   At sound advice from older voice?
I find it rude, your attitude,
   And must give tongue to scold you.
You won't be forever young,
   Life, in time, will mold you.
Oh lackaday! What's that you say?
   That I've <u>already</u> told you?"

Power Play

"Thirty kids, all on their own,
  No chaperone?
Not one adult on the spot?
  'Everybody's going'?
Well, you're not!"

Today's values can seem sleazy,
  New to us, and strange,
But parenthood's not easy,
  Some things *never* change.

Mamma, Tell Me..

Each morning I look out from bed
  And see the sky turn rosy red.
Then something strange shows up for me.
  The sun *pops up*, right from the sea,
And slowly, slowly, way up high,
  Climbs to the middle of the sky.
But wait! At night it slides down free,
  <u>Swallowed</u> <u>back</u> into the sea!
I just don't see how this can be,
  So Mamma, answer me this question..
Doesn't the sea get indigestion?

Surcease

There are days we should give in
   To the languid flow of time,
Just let go and feel the slow
   Pulse of the season's rhyme.

This kinship with the universe
   Will immerse you in its peace.
There is no sum within my purse
   Could purchase such release.

Shifting Time

Caught up in its towering power,
   I relished youth, its golden hour
Now vanished, slipped away.
   So little to show for its brief glow,
How far too short, its stay.

It does no good to grieve and yearn.
   What's gone is gone, will not return.
How can it be that I so lacked
   Awareness of this obvious fact?

And yet, and yet, I can't forget
   Joy at my current age.
A sense of peace without surcease,
   I love life at this stage!

I would not change things if I could,
   I've found that *all of life is good!*

No Denying

I can't deny, and must confess
    Dislike of the I.R.S.
What care they for my distress?
    We are not on terms of parity,
(They want *proof* for gifts to charity!)
    But if you make one small mistake
They almost burn you at the stake.
    Yet, believe me, you'd be stunned
If you received an earned refund.
    It's enough to make us sick,
The way they slap on fines that stick.
    (But watch them duck all situations
Requiring fines to *corporations.)*

I hope they all end up in Hādes,
    These nerds who pick on *little old ladies!*

Long-Gone Summer Day

The moon was oh so bright last night,
  And today, this glorious sun!
Not one single cloud in sight
  On a day so well begun.
I've time to try board-skating
  Before my tennis match,
And that golf course out there waiting
  Is a treat I need to snatch.

But oh I dearly love the beach,
  That arching one within my reach.
Too, with blazing sun prevailing
  On waters limpid blue,
I'm pining to go sailing,
  So what, oh what to do?

Somehow I'm going to do it all!
  Tomorrow might bring on a squall,
And golden days won't keep,
  With time now at my beck- and- call,
  Who needs sleep?

School of Life

With all that wisdom there inscrolled,
  Isn't it time I got enrolled?

Anticipation
(circa 1920's)

It's getting nearly Christmas
  And our house has got a shine.
The Christmas greens are hung up,
  The holly and the pine.
The Christmas lights are strung up
  And they all work just fine,
And Mom has polished all the brass
  And I've rubbed up the spoons,
And the only thing you hear at night
  Are jolly Christmas tunes.
Now Mom is making fruitcake,
  The darkest, richest kind.
(I'm chopping up the cherries,
  The nuts and citron rind.)
She's ready now to soak it,
  Needs half a cup of brandy,
And Dad says he just happens
  To have some good stuff handy,
(Soon I'll get to lick the spoon,
  And all that blissful batter.)
So the only thing that's lazy
  Is that old clock in the hall.
What *do* you think's the matter?
  Its hands just seem to crawl!

Confessions

When Eternity draws near,
  Do you rejoice, or do you fear?
Fear will never cross my mind,
  But oh, I'll rue what's left behind!
This teaches me just what is meant
  By that big word "ambivalent".

Zeal

When young, I thought to do it all.
  Filled with certitude,
Nothing could my ardor pall.
  With endless energy imbued,
Challenges were met, pursued.
  Yet with so much heaped upon my plate,
Aims and results did not equate.

  Life teaches us to trim our sails.
Attempt too much? A course that fails.
  Now as Time sounds out its knell
I aim for fewer things, done well.
  With countless worthwhile things to do,
Why bite off what we can't chew?

Election Reprise
(circa 2008)

Here's a fact that's all too true:
  If the *issues* we'd review,
Perhaps concede a point or two,
  And let our views expand,
Courtesy we'd then renew,
  Hostility disband.

This suggestion, can you best it?
  Four more years before we test it!

Take Note

Word to the wise:
Love reaches high,
  Up past the steeple.
It's not love that dies,
  But people.

Procrastination Problems

Those lowly tasks I ought to do
   Are dull. Can I eschew them?
I keep hoping someone new
   Will come along and do them.

What a banished hope. A myth!
   Undone chores now cause me woe.
If I had tackled them forthwith,
   They'd have vanished long ago.

I need to end this self-wrought grief.
   My course has been a source of sorrow.
What's required? A brand- new leaf.
   Watch me set to work *tomorrow!*

Invitation

I quell an urge to stun with poker
   Friends whose food is mediocre.
You who whine that dining bores,
   Come eat at my house,
      Not at yours!

As Ye Sow

Can we really all become
  What we aspire to be?
A bracing thought, and yet in sum
  It lacks reality.
Some steer clear of every shoal,
  Others won't attain their goal.
Yet if we continue vying,
  We contribute, just by trying.

I think we *should* shoot for the stars.
  If we reach half-way to Mars
We will have played a role.
  It's the sum of all its parts
That constitutes the whole.

Poetic Law

Let me make this clear:
All these ideas on your string?
Your noblest thought will disappear
If you don't seize it on the wing.
So hold it fast and make it last.
How?
Grab it <u>now.</u>

Choices

How be remembered? At what stage,
    Youth, mid-life, great age?
Since no-one alive my youth recalls,
    That early choice it thus forestalls.
Old age? How many folks are pining
      To be remembered, strength declining?

Now at last the picture clears...
    I would choose the middle years,
The time when life is shifting gears,
    And ambitions roil and stir.
Yes, that's the stage I would prefer.

But here's the thought that makes me quake:
    That choice will not be mine to make!

Revolt

Once, when striving to compete,
  Chinese ladies bound their feet.
But finding this not to their taste,
  Our grandmamas then laced the waist.
Next, mothers facing fashion hurdles
  Donned corsets, garter-belts and girdles.

This generation, heaven knows,
  Chose a worst foe to depose!
It faced the woes of panty-hose,
  Airless garments that deject us,
Cause us pain, almost bisect us.
  Too, this dreadful style insists
That we become contortionists,
  And struggle in unsightly throes
To squirm into those panty-hose!

But look about you. Take a glance
  At ladies, now all wearing pants.
In church or fête or on the street,
  Skirts are considered obsolete,
For those who think they're "in the know",
  Panty hose are now "de trop",
Emblems of a vanished past,
  And ladies, now iconoclast,
  Are shedding fast this *silken cast,*
Shouting out in piercing blast:
  "Free at last, free at last,
Thank God we are free at last!"

Lesson Learned

Adversity has many uses:
When trouble comes it introduces
   Each of us to ourself.
We learn to throw away excuses,
   Stow them on the shelf.

I, who view life from the rafters
   At my stage of existence,
Do not consider all disasters
   Immune to change, resistance.
At last we're starting to repair
   What we have done to once-pure air,
And have learned, I hope, to bar
   Headlong rushing into war.
Too, we can view with far more ease
   The ravages of dire disease.

We see the flowers each year, renewed,
   Thrust upward toward the sun,
Models for an attitude
   That says hard battles can be <u>won.</u>
Too, as in our gardens, we are loath
   To *weed out* acquisition-growth,
And the troubles we ourselves create
   Which we're too prone to blame on Fate.

What's needed? Not a sage or preacher.
 It's Nature we must take for teacher.
She's unique, without a rival.
 Her mantra's always been "survival".
We must learn, and all pay heed
 To wisdom we are sure to need.
****

Suggestion

Cocktail fêtes? They make me frown.
At stand-ups I must now sit down.
 Pinned to my chair, I try to snare
 Someone to sit beside me,
 But woe is me!
 Find a place to hide me!
(That's when this man who longs to flee,
 Decides he can't abide me.)

So you are right when you suppose
 That I have cocktail party woes
 Enough to spare.
 Oh, dear friends, dare I propose
 What's sure to be a winner?
Of course this fête requires a date,
 So I suggest a handsome guest
When you ask me home for *dinner!*

Lackaday!

I'm in disgrace too deep to face,
  I've looked in every single place,
In every cranny, nook.
  It does no good to even <u>pray</u>,
That book just up and went away,
  There's nowhere else to look!

Must I be cast into *perdition,*
  By a grim Librarian?
Was the book a First Edition?
  Should I try to gain remission
As <u>nona-genarian</u>?

Oh lost repose, oh sleep-deployment,
  So much grief, such brief enjoyment!
But <u>dear</u> Librarian, heed my sorrow,
  (There's still a book I need to borrow!)

Timing

What use to wail when I am gone?
  To no avail, forego it.
If in your heart you hold me dear,
  Let me know it *while I'm here.*

Arrival

Last night a mighty wind came up
   That rattled panes and eaves,
And today my garden, last week bright,
   Is choked with sodden leaves.
Too, all the oak trees clad in gold
Are shivering bare, there in the cold.

Yes, that's the way November came,
   Racing in, wind-borne.
She seeks approval and acclaim
   Despite the gardens, shorn.
Hers is a rocky road at best,
   A lonely one, forlorn ,
For Summer has been laid to rest
   While Autumn we still mourn.

Let-Down

Turn back, oh clock, turn back,
      Turn back!
(I'm coming down with Youth Attack.)
I'll skip along the sidewalk
   And jump across the cracks
When heading for the store to buy
   A rubber ball and Jacks,
And too, despite my facial wrinkles,
   An ice-cream cone with *chocolate sprinkles.*
(Too bad my age imposes ban.
   I'd love a game of Kick the Can.)

        ****

How lucky can I be? Hooray!
   My great-gran's coming for a stay,
And so we'll play and play and play
       All day!

        ****

My life is filled with major woes!
   (When she told me, I just froze!)
Oh dear, oh dear, here's what she chose..
   To play dress-up in adult clothes!

Nude Beach

If you go there seeking Cupid's shaft,
  All I can say is "You are daft!"
For I have noted, as a rule,
  That nothing so makes ardor cool
As naked bodies full of flaws
    To give us pause.
Let me confess my spirits flag
  At sighting all those parts that <u>sag</u>!

Thus Eve, (seeking visual *relief)*
  Plastered Adam with a big fig-leaf,
And he, whom we believe well-mated,
    Reciprocated.
Alas, they'd learned what's true, but sad..
  Folks <u>look</u> better when they're clad!

Eden Pillow-Talk

"Eve, for heaven's sake,
  Stop hob-nobbing with that snake!
He may *seem* an empty bubble,
  But Eve, believe me, he spells trouble!"

"Adam, don't under-rate your spouse.
  I know that reprobate's a louse,
But I can cope. I can grapple.
  All I want from him's an <u>apple</u>!"

"Oh my!
How I'd love an apple pie!
Perhaps you're right,
But keep that *creep* out of my sight.
Well, goodnight. Sleep tight, dear.
Mmmm!
Nice place, here."

Gender Gap

Women think an empty space
  Must be filled with talk,
An aspect of the human race
  That maketh men to balk.

In the Golden Silence they dictate,
  Ladies, hold your chatter.
Let the men orate and prate,
  (Their golf scores really *matter!*)

Decision

Oh dear, oh dear, it isn't fair! *
  My favorite shirt? Beyond repair.
   I couldn't wear it
    Anywhere!

Oh dear, oh dear, I do declare,
  What would happen
   Should I dare?
Guess I'd show up bare somewhere,
  And all the folks would glare
   And stare!

Must I huddle in my lair?
  This shouldn't make me
   Turn one hair.
I, with 'savoir faire' to spare,
  Will wear my tattered shirt
   With flair,
And show the neighbors
   I don't care!

** (Class challenge: to use rhyme-sound <u>air</u>
whenever possible in a piece that makes sense.)*

Tennis Tour

"Eye on the ball and follow through"
  (This lesson's been drummed into you.)
Applied to life I've found this rule
  Conforms to those in Sunday School.

The Way I See It

Outside my window, sea I spy,
   Hear surf, view sun and sky.
Inside, there's work I love to do,
   Dull duties now reduced to few.
I have old books, new D.V.D.,
   Well-loved friends who come to tea.
Thus life for me has precious worth.
   How far from dull I find this earth!

Are these the things, do you suppose
   That turn my views "couleur de rose"?

Limits

Life is something
I love madly.
All my errors I view
Sadly.
Patience? Something
Practiced badly,
And fools I'll never suffer
Gladly.

Tell Me

Isn't this what
It's all about,
To give back more to life
Than we take out?

Showdown

"Mom, we find it so outrageous,
  Not to mention, bold,
That you are still *flirtatious.*
  Don't you know you're old?"

"Well, goodness gracious!
  As if I needed to be told!
Sorry, kiddos, if it vexes,
  But the Lord, in His design,
Made *two separate sexes,*
  And I'm enjoying mine!

Double Blessing

God has made a wondrous gift
  To Man.
Gold, we can't take with us.
  Love, we can.

Yet at the journey's finish
  Bear this truth in mind.
The gift will not diminish
  The love we leave behind.

Largesse

Alas, our Earth's in trouble deep,
   We've "miles to go before we sleep".   *
Not even beasts despoil their lair.
   Will we clean, clear up, repair,
      Renew, replace
What we have done to Earth's dear face,
   Or will we shrug, and join the chorus?
(*"Someone else will do it for us."*)

The sands of life are running through,
   Our help, long overdue.
 No trouble is too much to take
   When life itself is what's at stake.

Antidote to worries, care,
   Love of life's a form of prayer.
A thanks for all we earthlings share,
   A death-knell to despair.

How our errors sting and smart!
   Add them, they soar off the chart.
Love of life will strength impart.
   Miles to go? It's time to start!

* *Robert Frost:. "Stopping By the Snowy Woods"*

Tanglewood

The music, oftentimes sublime,
  Played second place to *crime*.
What's this about? Some talked
    Throughout.
Without a doubt I should have shouted
  To all those louts outdoors,
" Quiet, you spouting bores!"

Yet, fraught with courage weak as custard,
  My reprimands were never mustered.
Still filled with rage I cannot quell,
  I want them forced to scream and yell
    In hottest hell!

Prayer

Old age can encase us,
  Wrap us in a shell.
Let it not erase us,
  Entrap us in its cell.

To feel the pain of others,
  That power must not abate,
And since all men are brothers
  Help us to relate.

More Questions

Are there those among us
  Who have never known defeat?
(Should this prove to be the case,
  Their lives are incomplete.)
Don't we know we'll someday walk
  On both sides of the street?
Don't we need a Higher Power
  To sustain, and give us aid?
Is a lemon not required
  To give us lemonade?
If we've done an unkind deed,
  Does not our conscience burn?
Don't we place most value
  On the things we've had to earn?
Don't we still continue
  To strive to grow, to learn?
Is it not its contrasts
  That give existence, drama?
Why put to life a period?
  God prefers a comma!

Span of Time

"Over the river and through the woods" *
   To Grandmother's house they came.
(I'm giving you the true straight goods.
   Soon that house didn't look the same!)
Boisterous troops gave shouts and whoops,
   Ran to the attic for old toys.
   Oh my Lord, the noise!

Worry not, she kept her poise,
   Gave big hugs to girls and boys,
A taffy pull, a popcorn ball,
   Her special stuffing, good things all.
This Gran looks back to those Novembers
   Now long gone, and she remembers..

To that Gran she owes a debt,
   One she's not apt to forget.
In her flat, a wee bit small,
   How she's welcomed each and all,
Rolled up the rugs, with hugs for all,
   Thrust out taffy, popcorn ball,
Found she's loved and been beguiled
   By every noisy, boisterous child.

Yes, things work out as she intended.
   Those noisy kids? How well they blended!
That torn couch? It can be mended!

*Lydia Marie Child. (1884)

Sought

If you live to reach great age,
   How empty sometimes seems the stage.
Though younger friends you hug to heart,
   They won't share your time-chart.
Your memories are to them, closed doors.
   (Theirs don't reach back as far as yours.)
What you need's a John or Mary,
   A friend who's your contemporary,
Who can, at times when life seems sunny,
   Recall Depression's lack of money,
Name old cars, old movie stars,
   Remember empires, kings and czars,
Bear the scars of <u>two</u> World Wars,
   And cherish values, the myriad ways
We found to cope, in long-gone days.

Today we deem our lives first- rate.
   We move about. We circulate,
Do our part, participate.
   Grandchildren keep us up to date,
We use computers, Dead, the slate.
   Yet sometimes, as we view the frey,
Our thoughts turn back, begin to stray.
   Bi-sected, we then *straddle the fence.*
Confused by Past and Present Tense,
   How we veer and how we cavil!

Oh for a <u>peer</u> to help unravel
   The complex, dual road we travel!

The Long Road

Oh the rhythm, oh the rhyme,
  Oh the endless flow of Time,
The future, ours to mold!
  To adventure never loath,
Joy and hope, we had them both.
  How unreal was "old"!

Life can never hope to teach us
  If its growing-pains we spurn.
Time eventually will leach us
  If deaf ears we turn.
Yet slowly, slowly, wisdom stirs,
  And, if tragedy occurs
We begin to see that even pain
  Can yield a form of gain.

As our universe expands
  We learn to welcome life's demands.
"The last, for which the first was made" *
  Then finds us joyous, unafraid..
We slow the pace, face and embrace
  Our kinship with the human race.

Robert Browning

Iraq

Almost every day we learn
  Of soldier heroes, dead, unsung,
Who, like figures on a Grecian urn,
  Will be forever young.

To no avail, the prayerful waiting.
  Do families find this <u>compensating?</u>

Try It

Forgiveness is a blessing
  That enriches giver.
Nothing's so depressing
  As anger in one's quiver,
So if you have a fraction,
  Even just a sliver,
Extract it. Watch the action!
  The brook becomes a river.

Switch

Now that 95's my age
  Why do folks expect a sage?
Alas, too prone to jovial quips,
  No wise words pour from my lips.

Don't you agree it's sad to see
  Such a self-inflicted fix?
Surely they'll <u>wise up to me</u>
  Before I'm 96!

Count On It

Life's a gamble, no sure thing,
  Times of wailing, hurts that sting,
Joyous days of caps to fling,
  Sunsets and the afterglow,
Volcanoes that erupt,
  Shifting winds that veer and blow,
Involving change abrupt.

There's so much more we must explore,
  The complicated mixture
Of the trivial, the profound,
  The warp, the woof, the texture
Of life, each daily round.
  (Will we bring our ship to shore
Or will we run aground?)

I guess, when all is said and done,
  That's why life is so much fun!

Pearl Beyond Price

"I don't care if <u>both</u> knees bleed!
  All these flowers were raised from seed.
Too, heed the blisters got from weeding.
  But no, I'm not *thinking* of seceding.
Of course you cannot <u>buy</u> my cottage!
  All your gold? A mess of pottage!"

Overview

The separate periods of our lives?
  Each one is distinct.
It's only as we near the end
  We realize they're linked.
The child you <u>were</u> determines
  The adult you'll become,
And all life's various pieces
  Add up to its sum.

It's at the last you understand.
  Of course your actions had a hand,
But life's not random. It was planned.

Dirge

Oh dear, it's now become my fate,
  (one that my children taunt,)
To be hopeless, out –of-date.
  What I see on my T.V.,
All those things they flaunt,
  I'd never learn to operate,
    And do not want.

"Reality" Show

It will point a finger your age,
  (But do you care, at this late stage?)
You rue the loss, the fearful waste,
  Where has it gone, good taste?

Don't be a T.V. stooge or maven,
  Shut it off, not forced to look.
There is refuge, there is haven,
  Find it in a book!

Guarantee

What worse thing
  Can disrupt slumber?
A loud phone ring,
  " Wrong number".

Warning

When writing, yes, I close my curtain,
  Not good company, for certain,
For I am just a hopeless dunce
  Who cannot do *two things at once.*
  You, though friend I deem first –rate,
  Can make my thoughts evaporate.
Recall, when you "drop in" to talk,
  I'm one who can't *chew gum and walk*!

Sea Song

Oh for the swooshing and splashing,
   The sibilant sounds of the sea,
All of the crashing and smashing,
   The waves that are dashing at me!
Give me the surging, the sighing,
   The murmurs as soft as can be.
Perhaps I could put up with dying,
    If only I died by the sea.

False

    The word I heard?
  "Old age is filled with woes."
     Yet I have found its joys resound
     At each day's close.
  A poet wrote about "the best",
    Said it was "yet to be".
  I disagree, for I avow
    The best is <u>now.</u>

Thanks

I'm returning to what's part of me,
  For Man, we know, came from the sea.
Most of my life's been lived near water.
  I'm bound to it, as if by mortar.
The crash of waves? My favorite chord.
  How blessed I am to hear it, Lord!

Tally

Each day I write a single line,
   On it affix my name.
"How has this day defined me?
   Has it wrought pride, or shame?"

If toward the latter it's inclined me
   And I've not reached my aim,
Dear Lord who designed me,
   I've just myself to blame.
Make me take a look inside,
   (Perhaps I'll swallow all that pride!)

Ahead

Blessed with zest for living,
   To most health woes immune,
I greet each day, it's fair to say,
   Rejoicing, and in tune.
So be sure I won't "go gentle *
   Into that good night"
Nor is it accidental
   That the prospect holds no fright.

* *Dylan Thomas*

Comparison

Oh world that I'll be leaving soon,
  Let there be sun and star and moon,
And stream and rounded hill,
  And marigold and daffodil,
And oh dear Lord, the rose!
    May they flourish there somewhere
      When I reach repose.
Too, birds of course, there at the source,
    And breeze and trees and honey-bees,
And storms of fearful force.

      One thing I know..
    If I find them there, up where I go,
They won't surpass *what's here below.*

Balance

Unsatisfied by status quo,
   Into knowledge I must delve,
For I, like Cinderella, know
   The clock will soon strike twelve.
Zest for quest of lore's essential
   If we're to reach our full potential,
Yet before each day is done
   I must include a dose of fun,
An hour or two spent in the sun.
      Now doubts assail.
Which predilection will prevail?

For threaten me with jail or rod,
   I'll still insist on pleasure,
And give to labor just a nod.
   (This, my use of leisure.)
Yet aspirations always soar,
   Aims undiminished,
So Lord, don't tally up the score
   Until my journey's finished.

For we must always strive to render
   Thanks for life and all its splendor.
I can't disclaim my aim to strive.
   (Is this why I'm still alive?)

Welcome Guest

Hark to news I here impart:
  In my youth, a bluebird
  Nested in my heart,
And I, a stranger to despair,
  Know the bluebird
    Still dwells there.

Gratitude

I've traveled far, to distant places,
  Met folks of varied talents, races,
Viewed the treasures of those climes,
  Used my aptitude for rhymes.

The infants that I held to heart
  Are grown, contributing their part.
Many a golden hour's been spent
  Planting flowers to heart's content.
Many a book has stretched my mind,
  Many a friend's been wined and dined.
Convinced that all things work toward good
  I see us inch toward brotherhood.

Never one inclined to worry,
  I've long outlived the hurry, scurry.
My blessings grow, they never cease,
  Certainty has yielded peace.

Query

Why is it that the mind reverts
  To what is good, forgets the hurts?
I believe, (of course it's guessing,)
  That this might be life's major blessing.
It's the picnic, gala ball,
  Or important victory I recall,
And hours with children, much loved friends,
  While Time, the thief, wipes out deep grief,
And all the loveliest memories <u>blends.</u>

Why this happens I don't know.
  I just thank God that it is so.

Seeker

Enjoying life, still filled with zest,
   I'm embarking on a quest
To find out why I've been so blessed,
     Never put to major test.
I have friends who from the start,
  Have enriched their niche within my heart.
Great-grandchildren fill my arms,
  Poems still descend in swarms,
    My garden glows with roses.
So though I thank a kindly Fate,
  (No-one could term me an ingrate,)
I must find, despite life's charms,
    The goal that it discloses.

   I think it clear that we are here
    A purpose to fulfill,
And from life's feast, what I want least?
    To leave an unpaid bill.
I bow of course to higher will.
  But before I climb that final hill,
    Hurry, Lord! I'm waiting still!

Hymn to Life

Boredom's always been a thing
　　I fail to understand.
Activities outside the home
　　Accept my helping hand.
I seek good conversation,
　　And on new ideas thrive,
Love flowers, music, people,
　　Rejoice at being alive.
So hear my hymn of praise to life,
　　I've loved mine to the hilt,
　Have had fair share of fun and care,
　　Of approbation, guilt.
I've known success, and too, despair,
　　It's been a crazy quilt,
And yes, have laid my feelings bare,
　　But for every tear I've spilt
I've found a way to mend, repair
　　The balance and the tilt,
　Rejoicing that my fun's not done,
　　That I still know joy and lilt.
Too, I hew to point- of- view
　　That every day brings challenge new,
A chance to sing, to join the chorus,
　　Of awe at wonders set before us.

That's why I lift my voice in praise.
　　Oh life, how wondrous are your ways!

Conclusion

When we grow old and wise and staid,
   We envy youth, so un-afraid.
We learn we can't destroy or seize
   The dreaded sword of Damocles.

What lessons did my long life teach?
   That we must not give up, resign,
Or cease to strive, to hope, to reach,
That our Creator in His grand design
   Has further plans in store,
That we should not worry or repine,
   But relish gifts galore,
And that His hand, reached out for mine,
   Will guide me safe to shore.

Table of Contents

Titles and First Lines

C

D

H

I

J

N

O

P

I shall rise up in my coffin
Beset by surging rhyme.
Quick! A piece of paper
One LAST time!